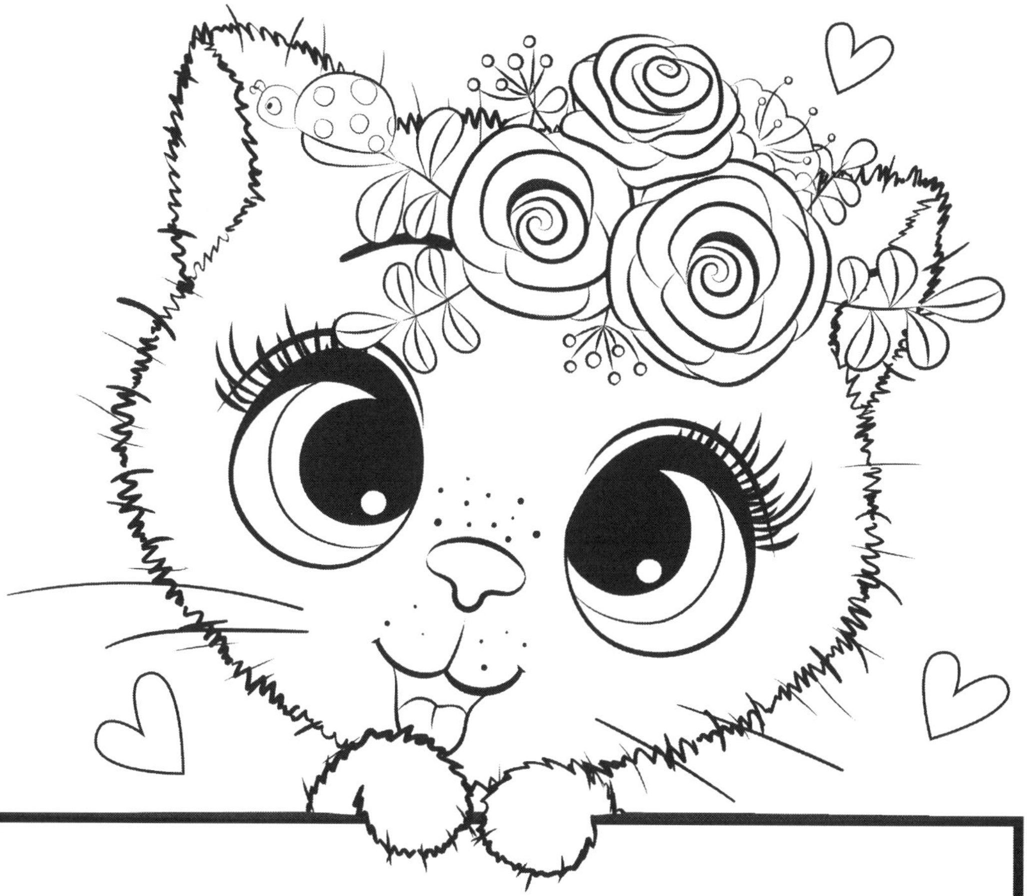

THIS BOOK BELONGS TO:

Ruby

Golden Age Press

VISIT US ONLINE:
WWW.GOLDENAGEPRESS.COM

ISBN-13 : 978-1955421065

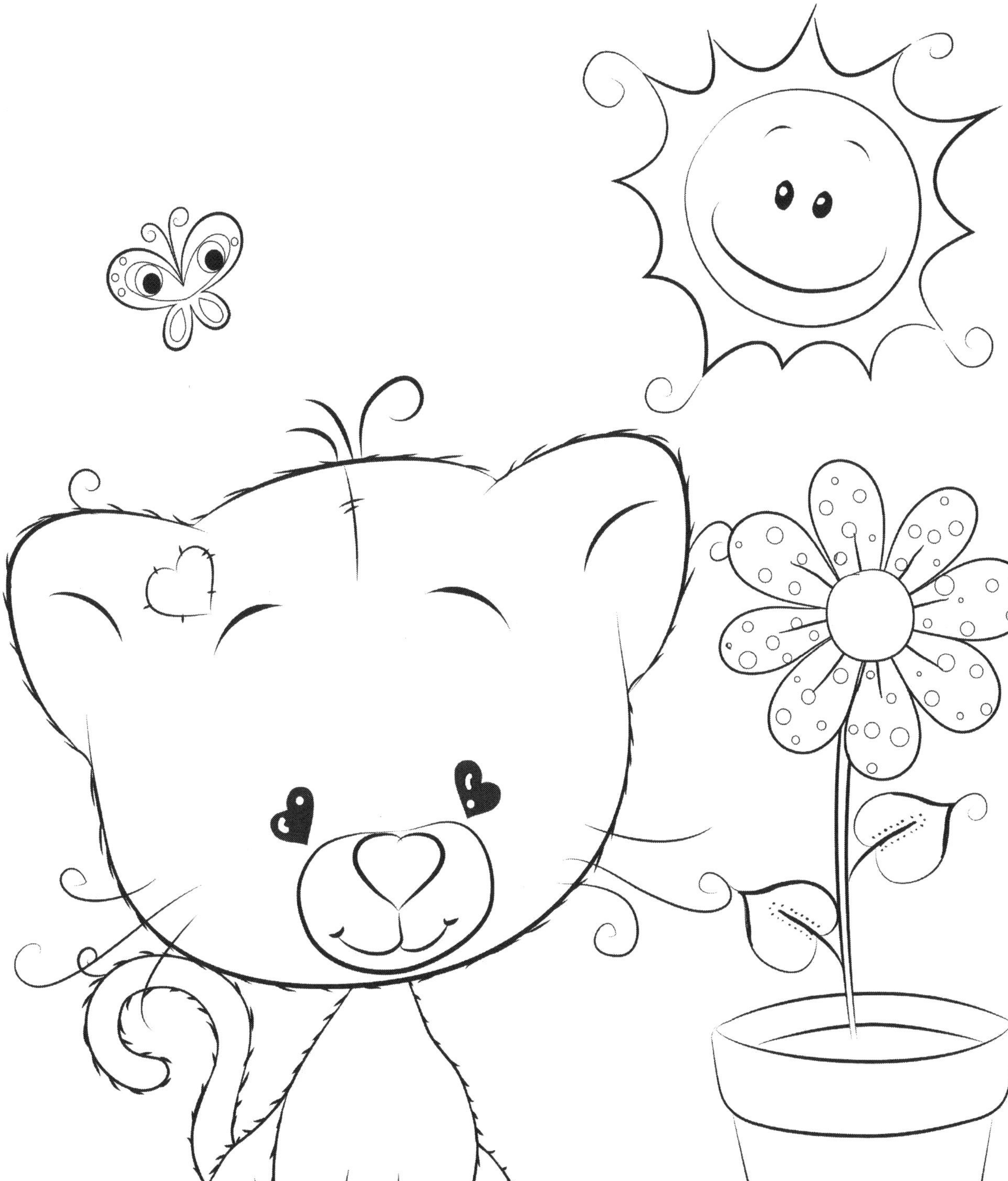

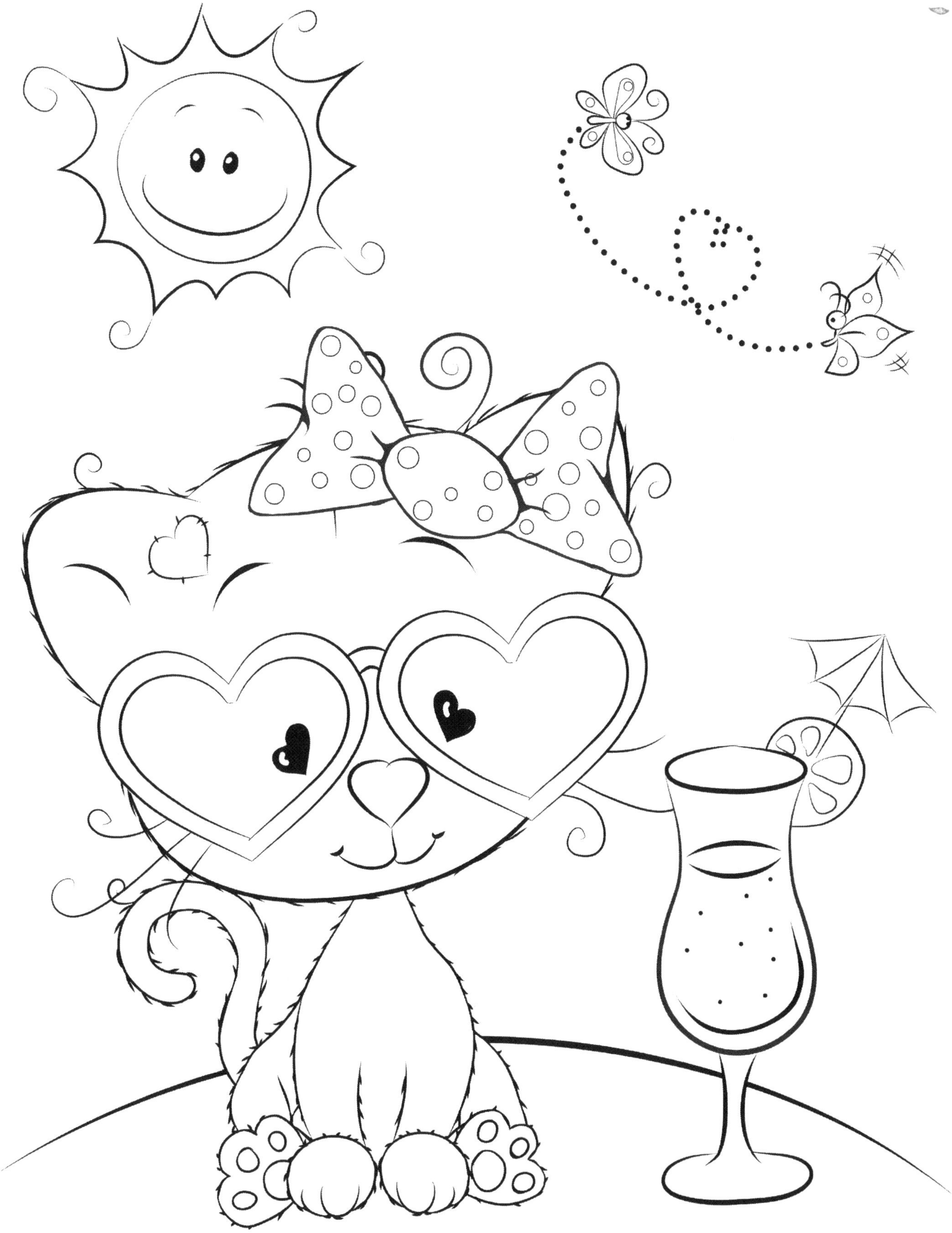

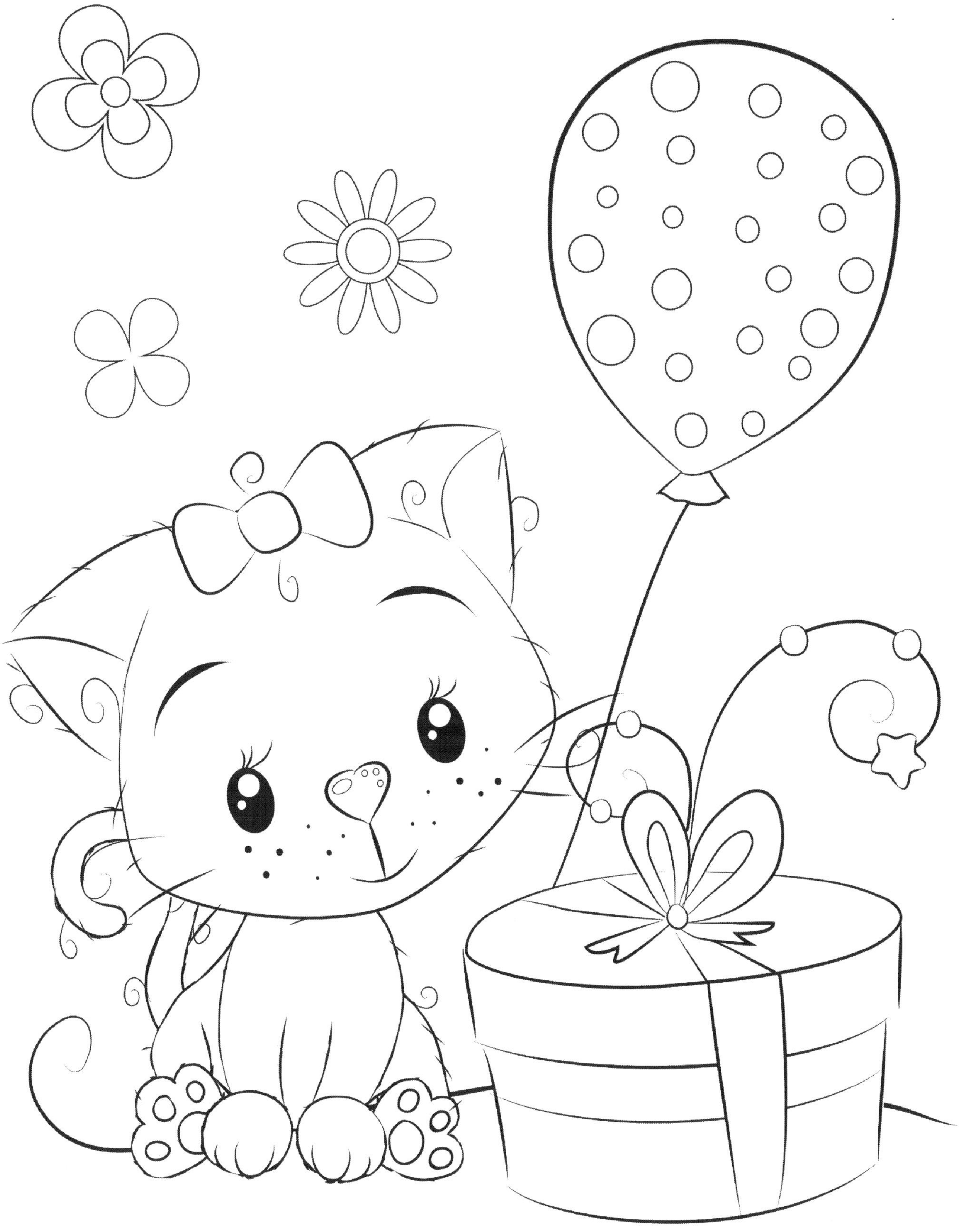

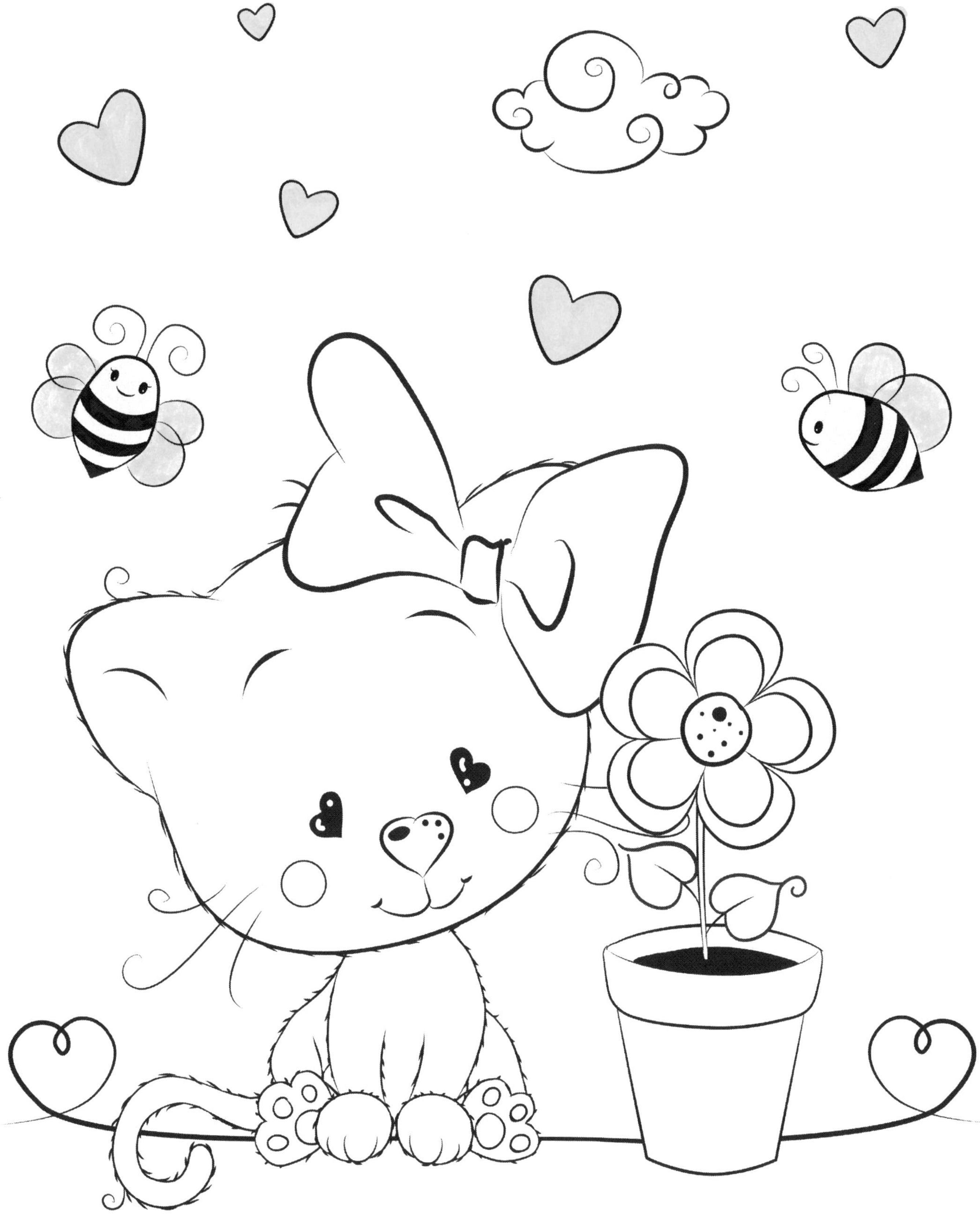

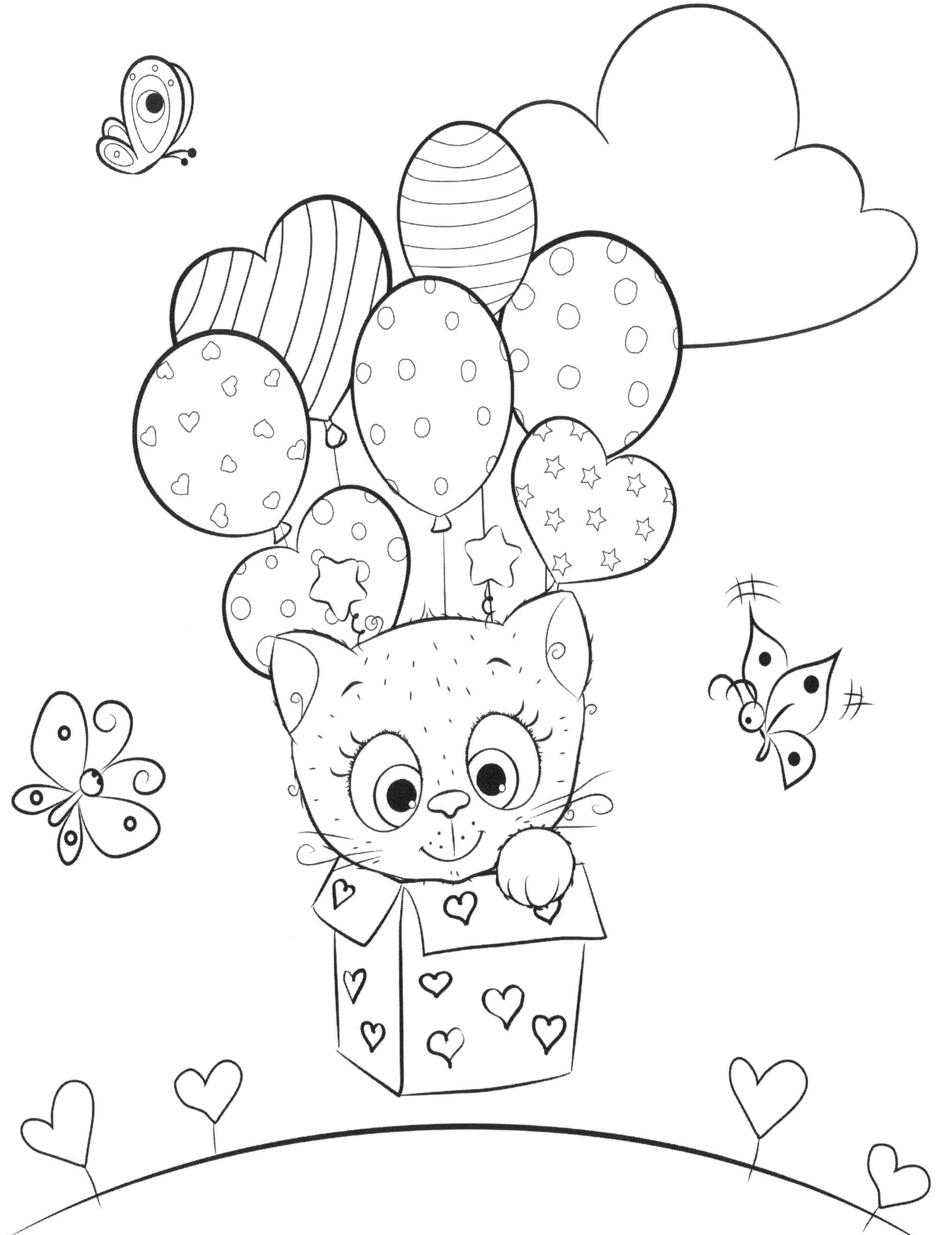

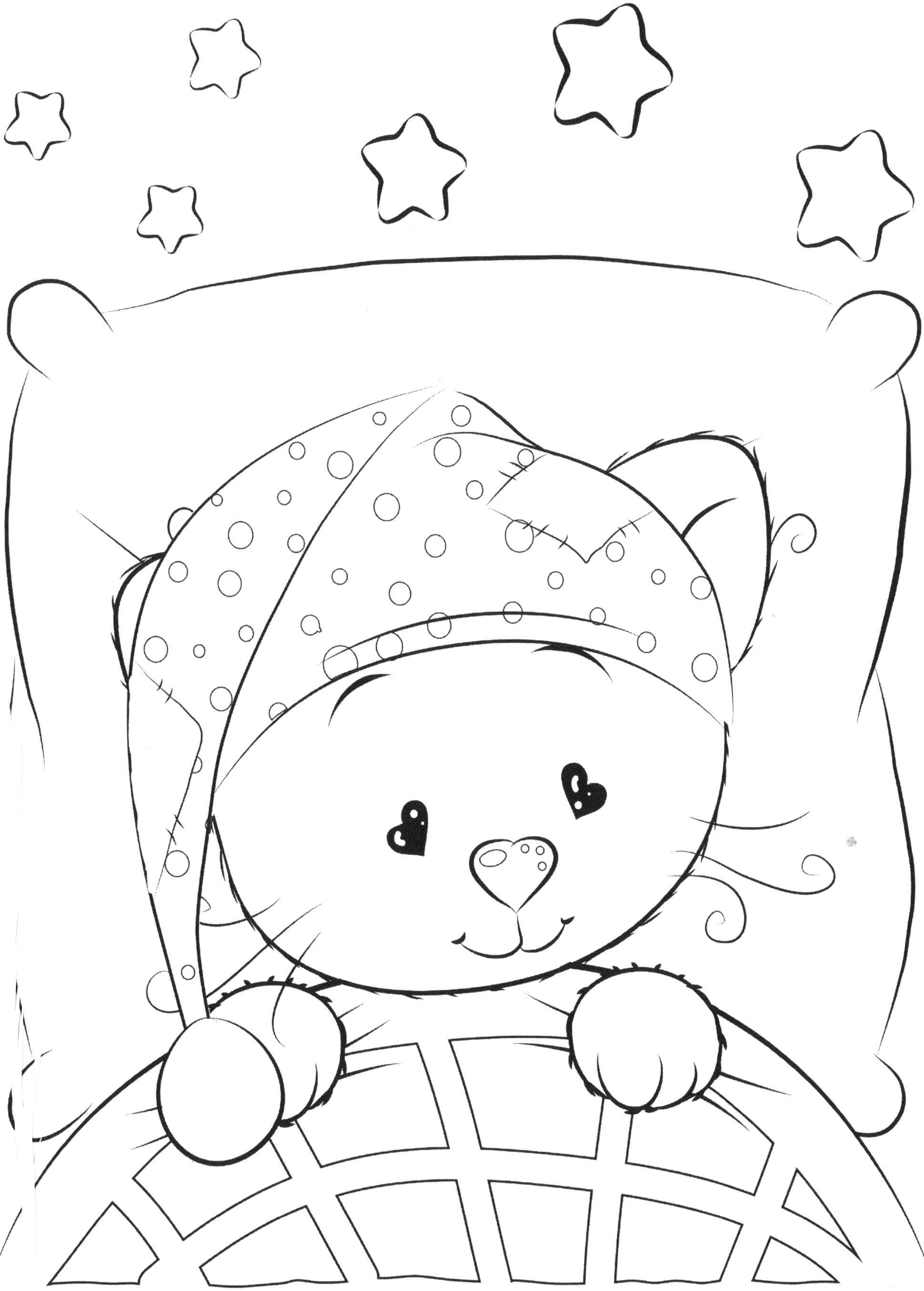

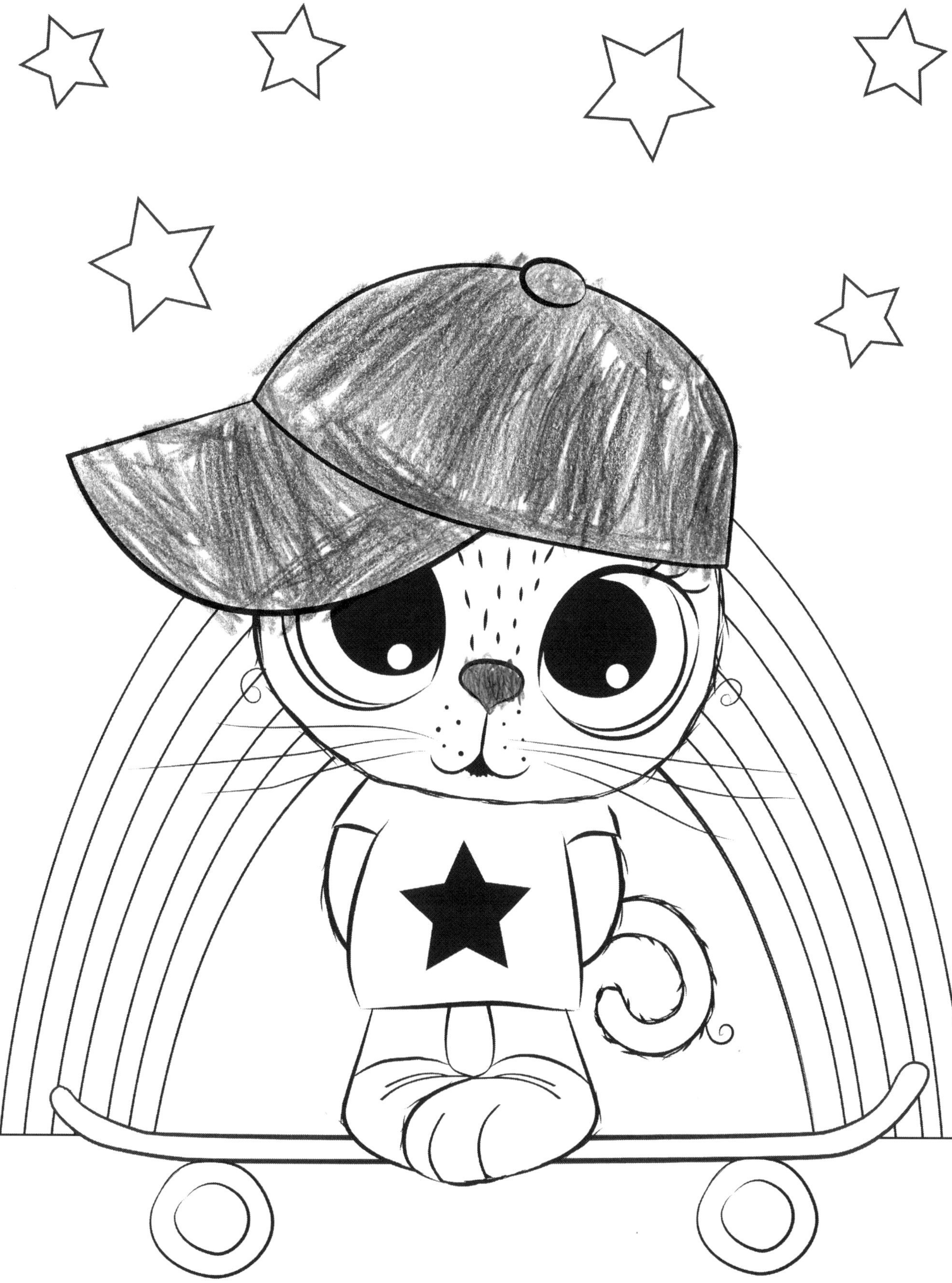

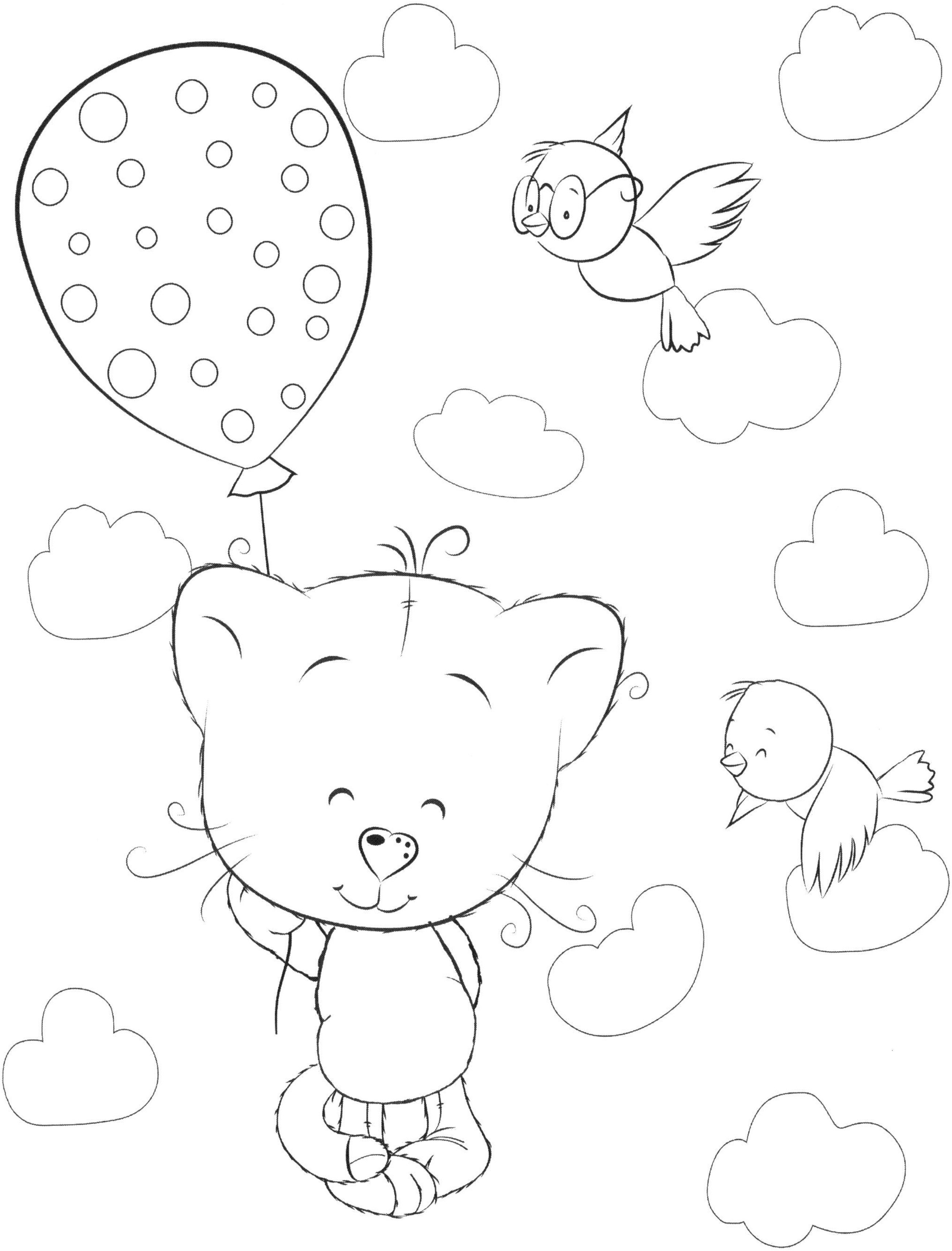

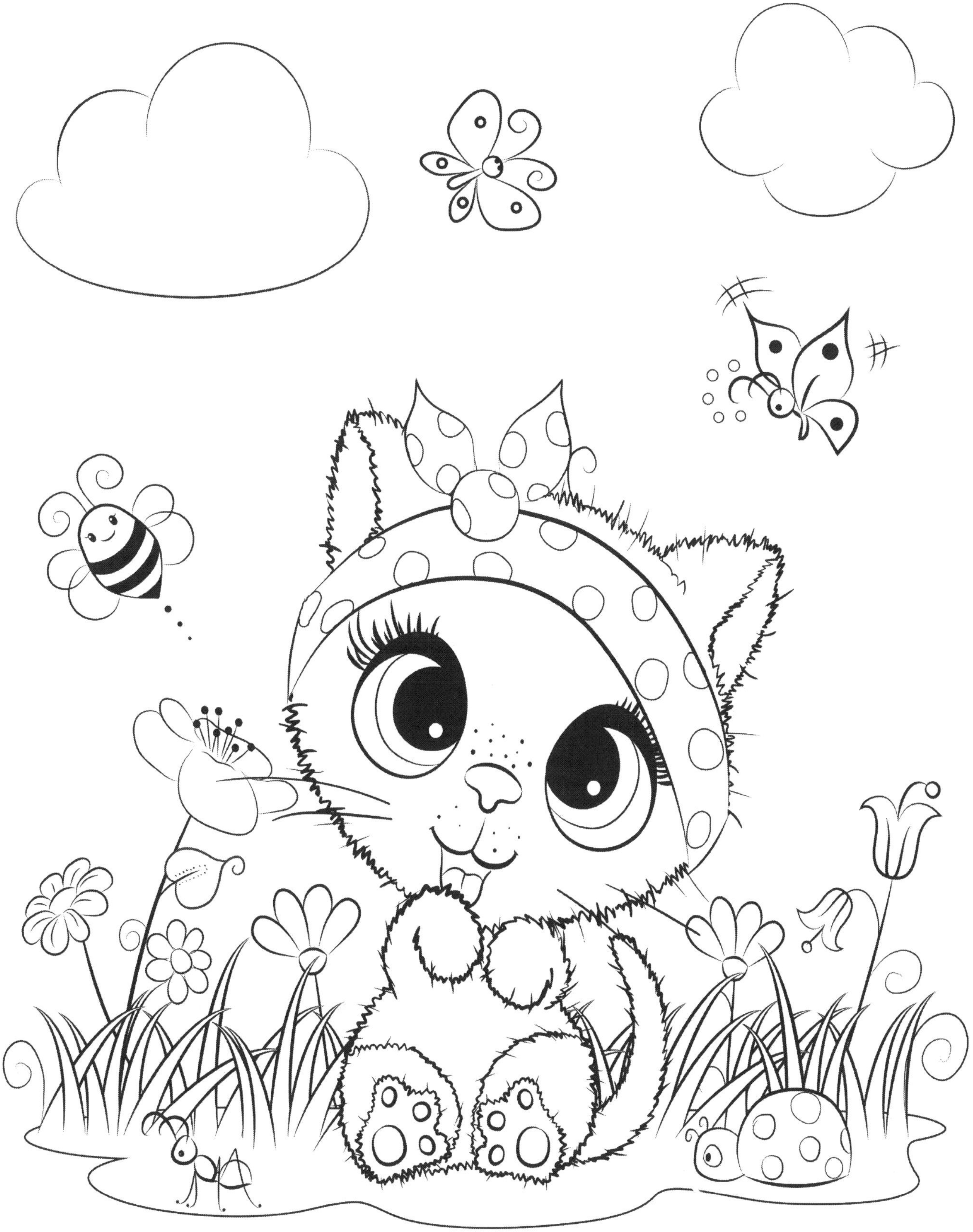

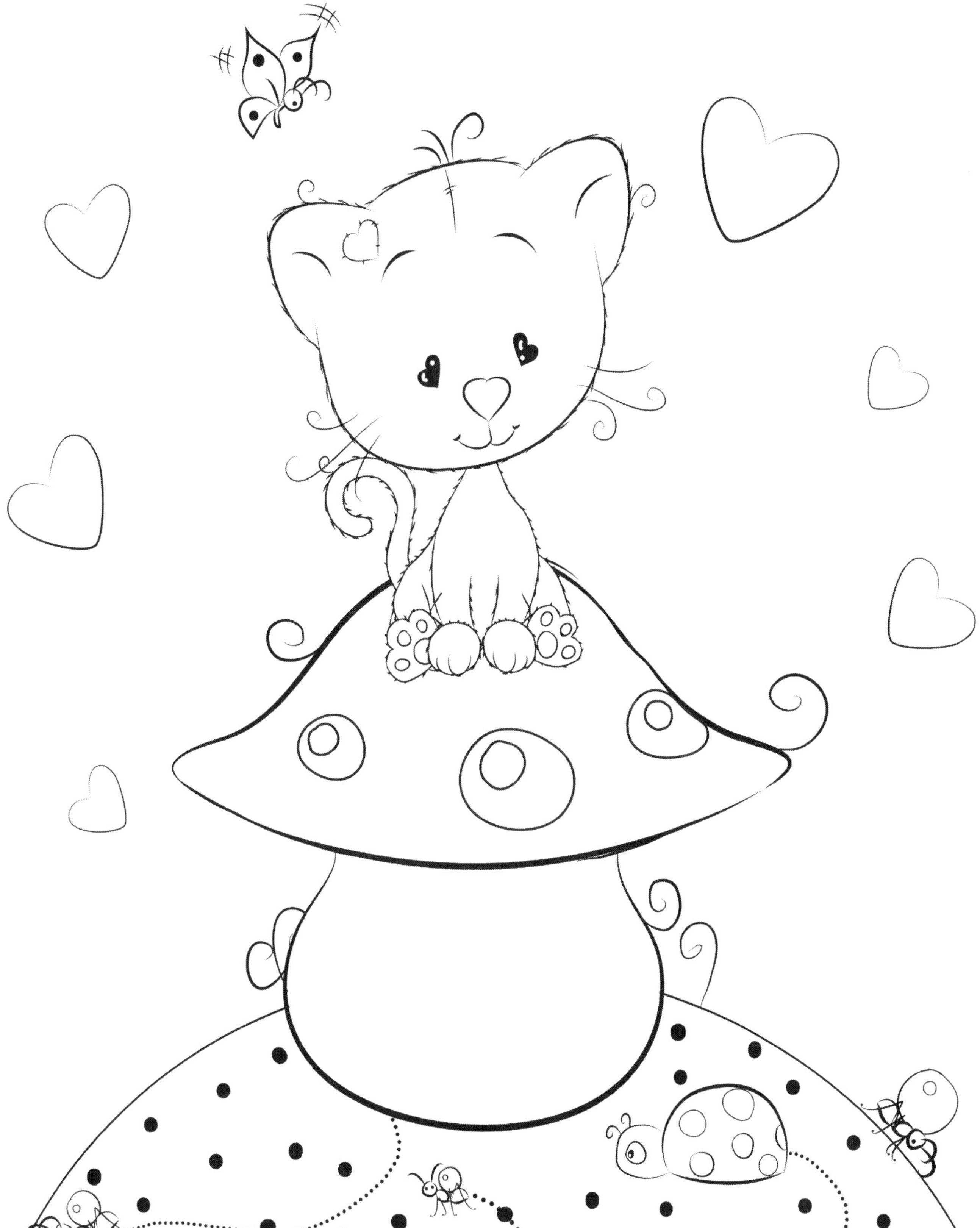

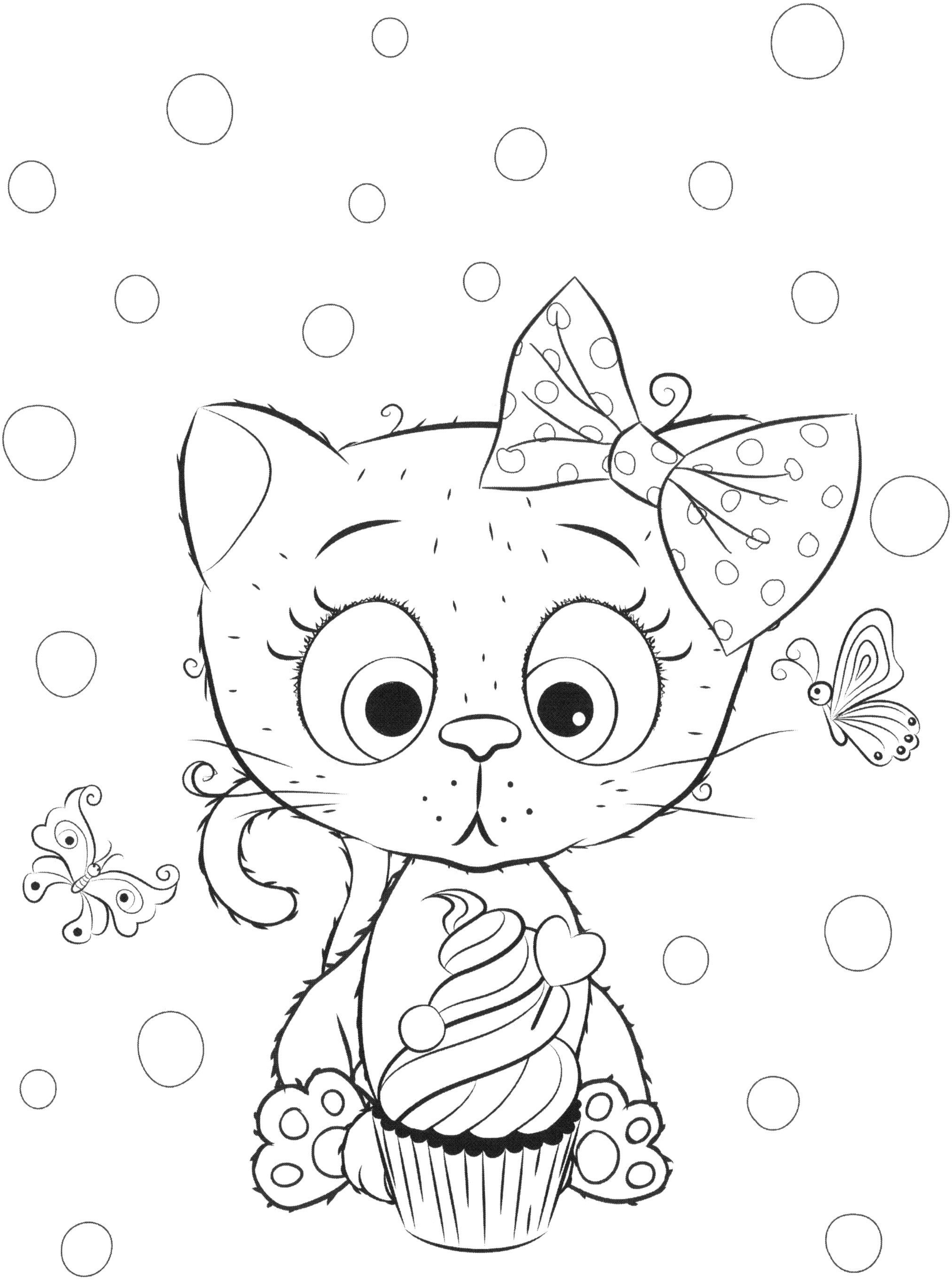

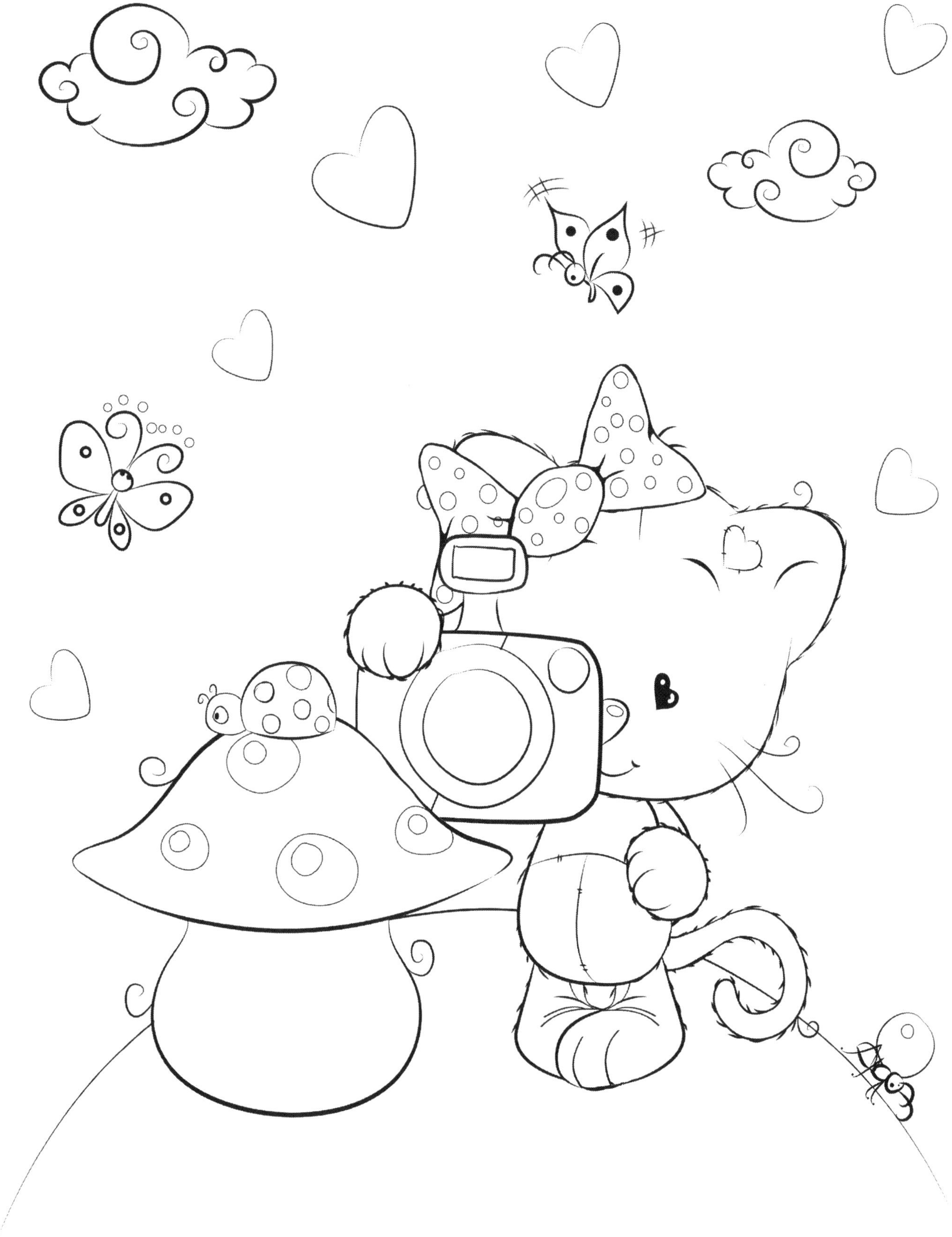

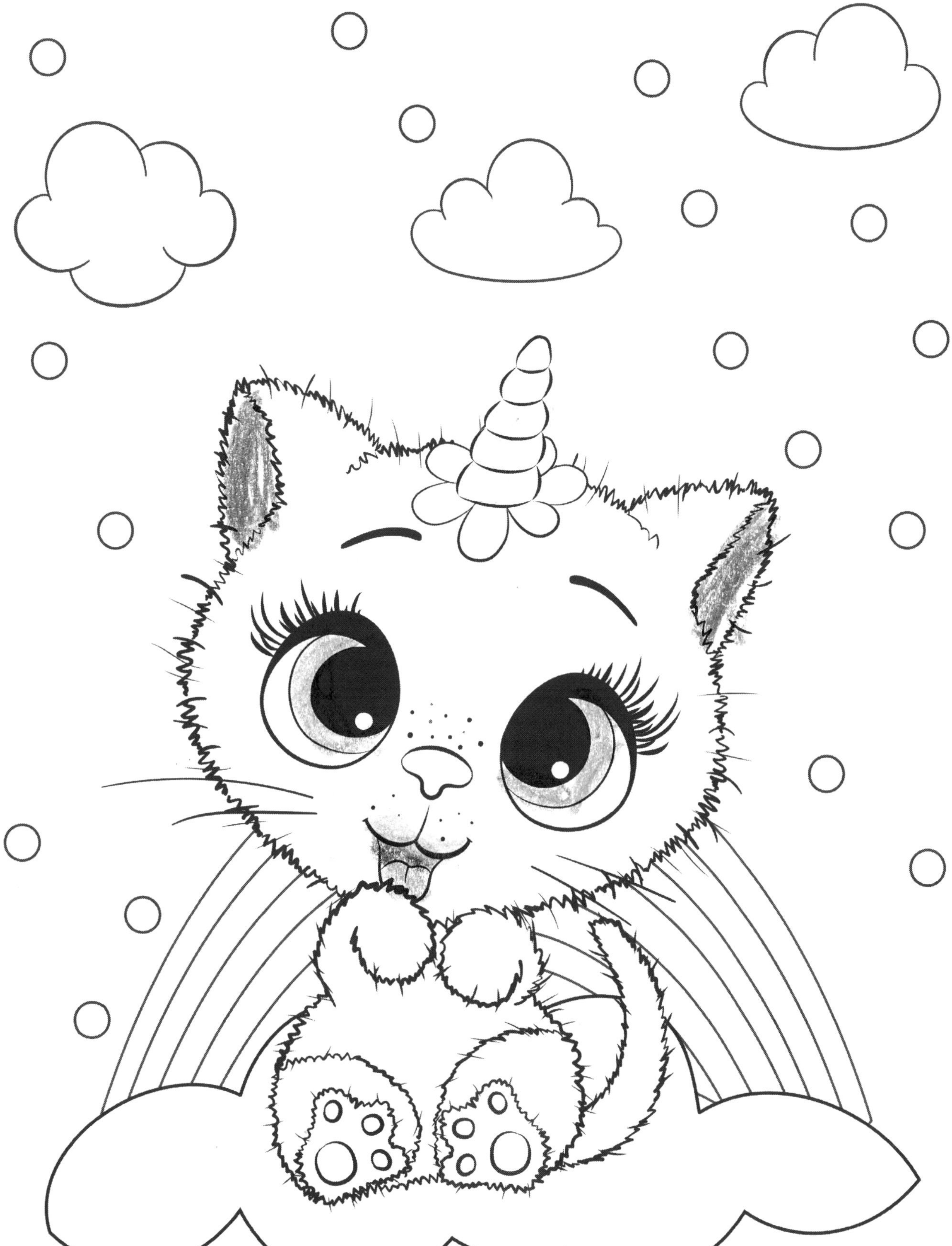

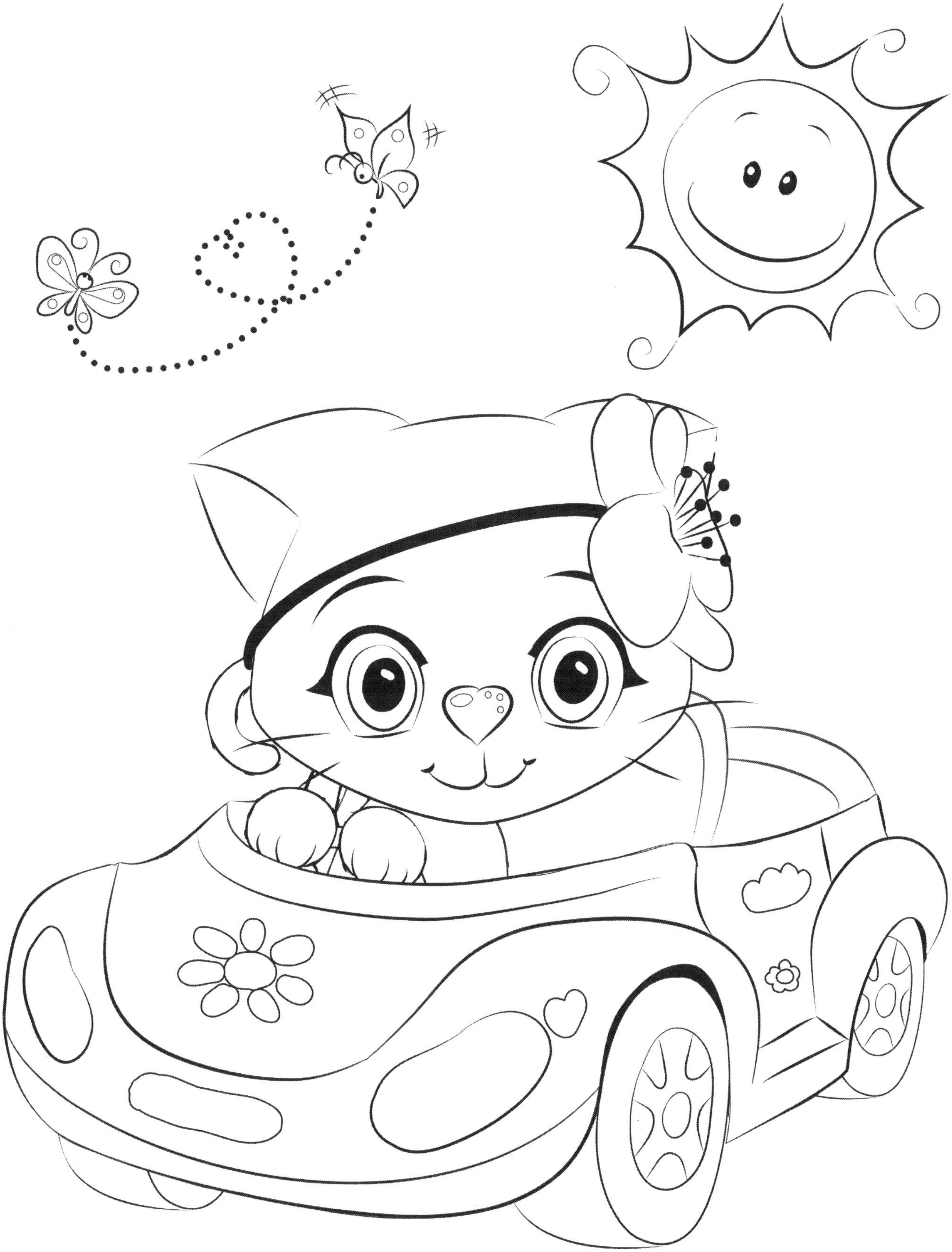

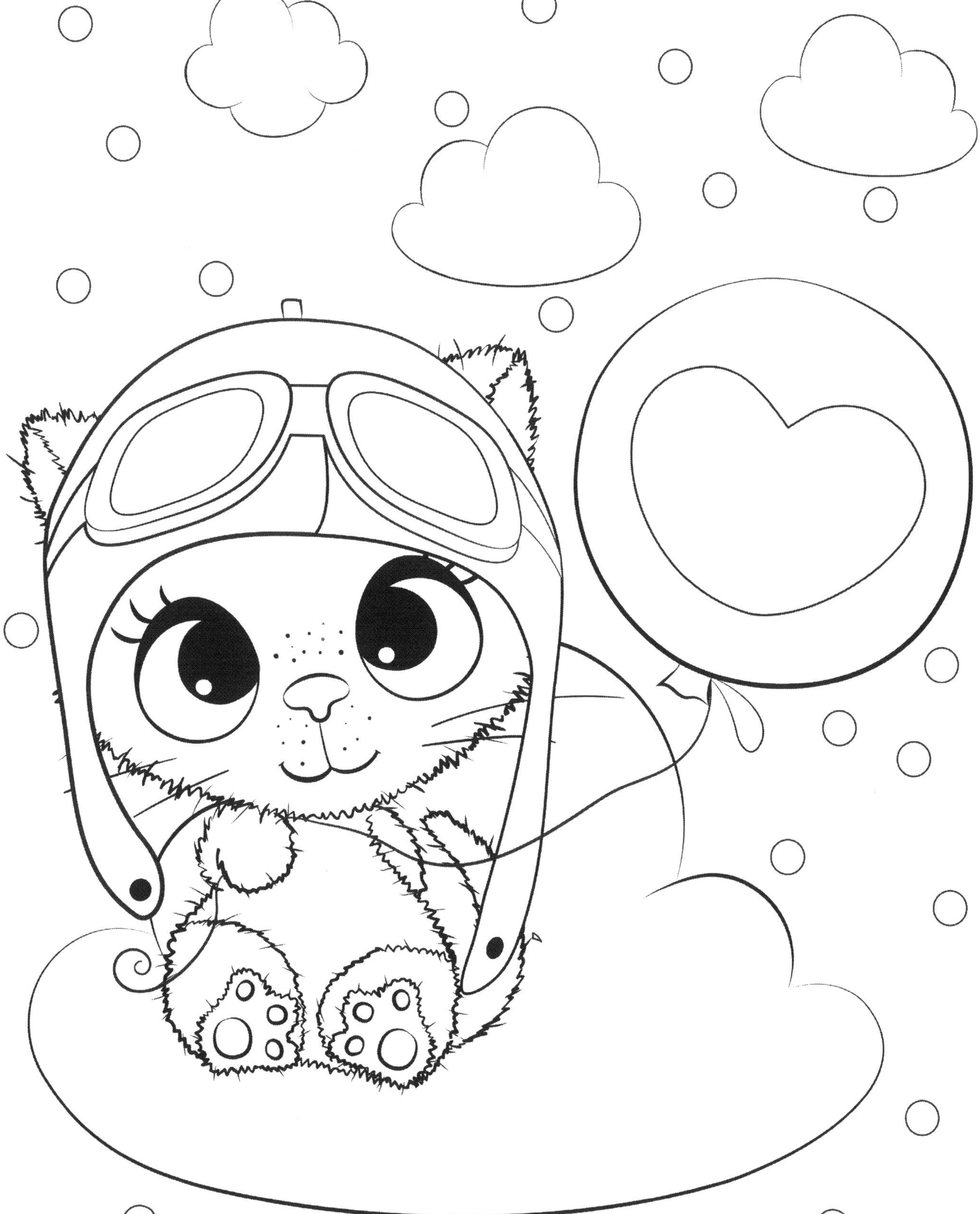

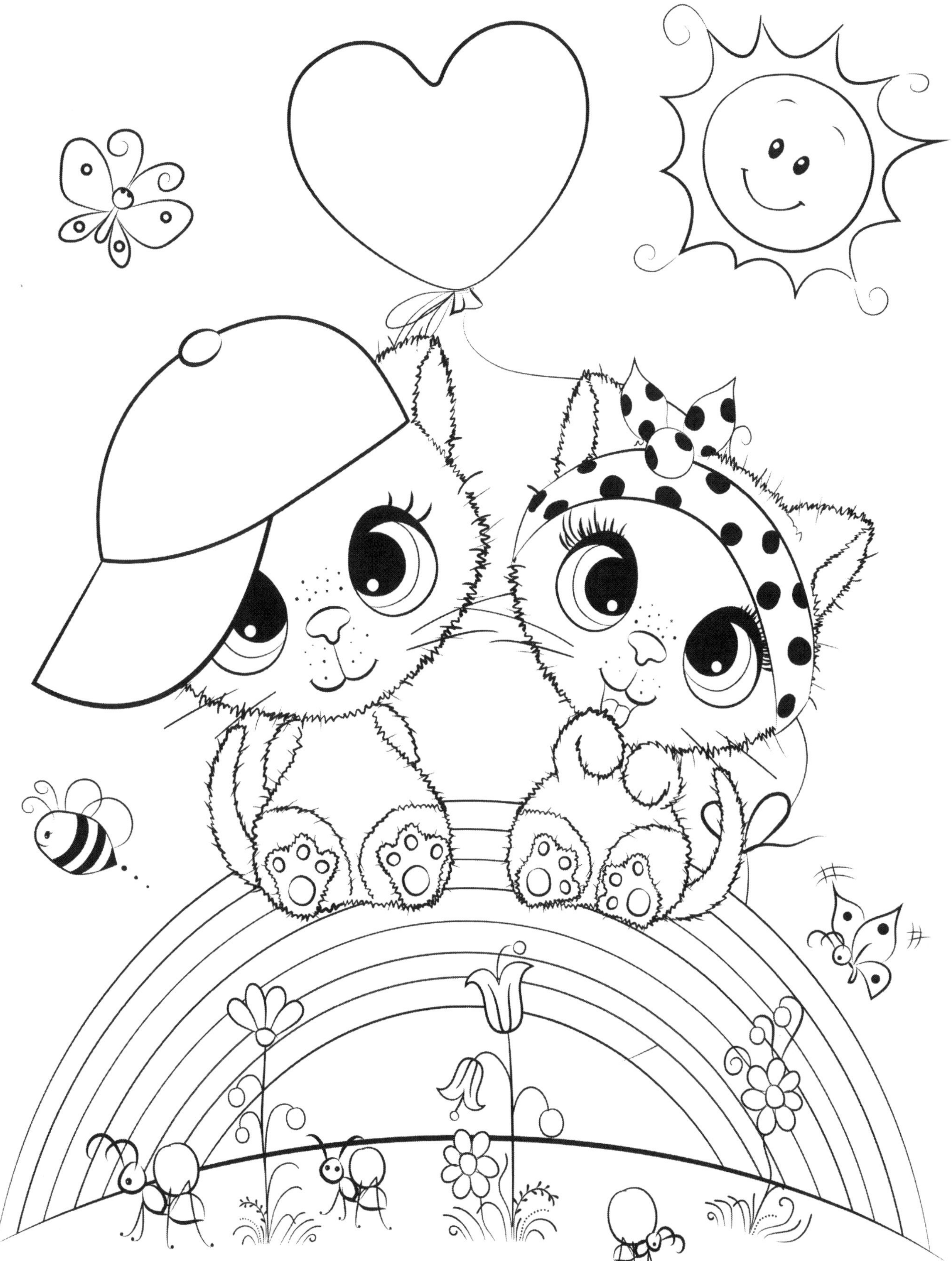

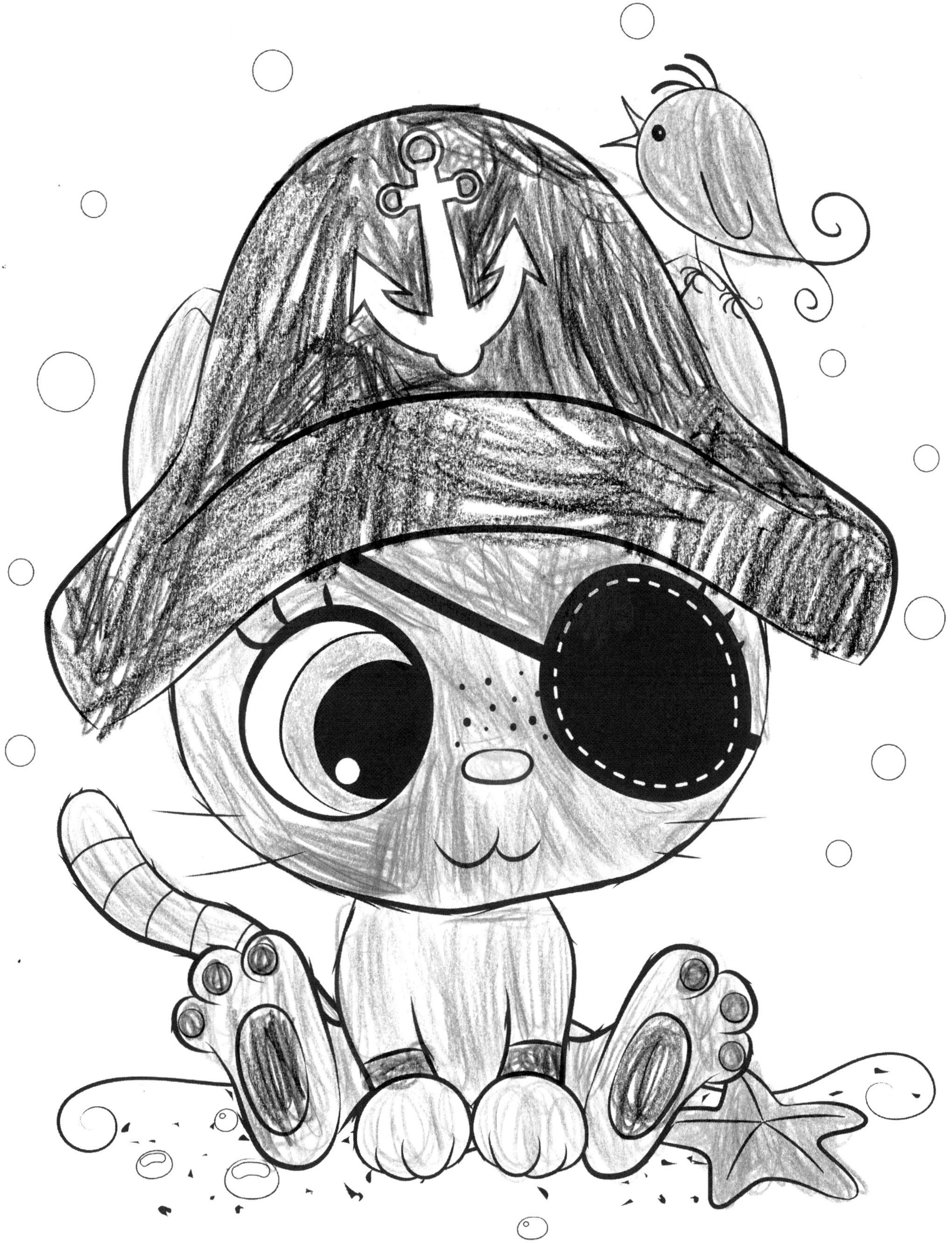

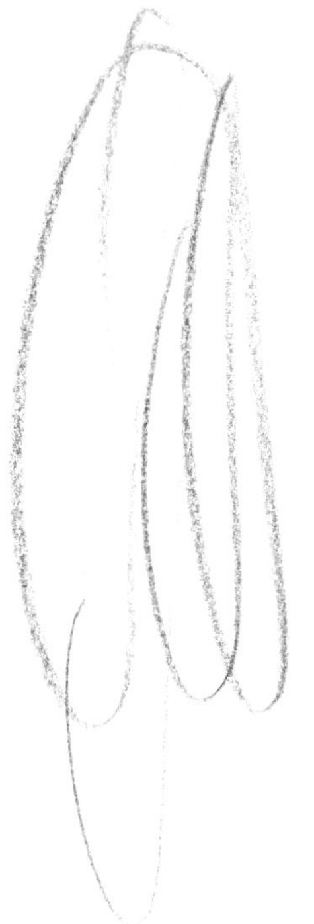

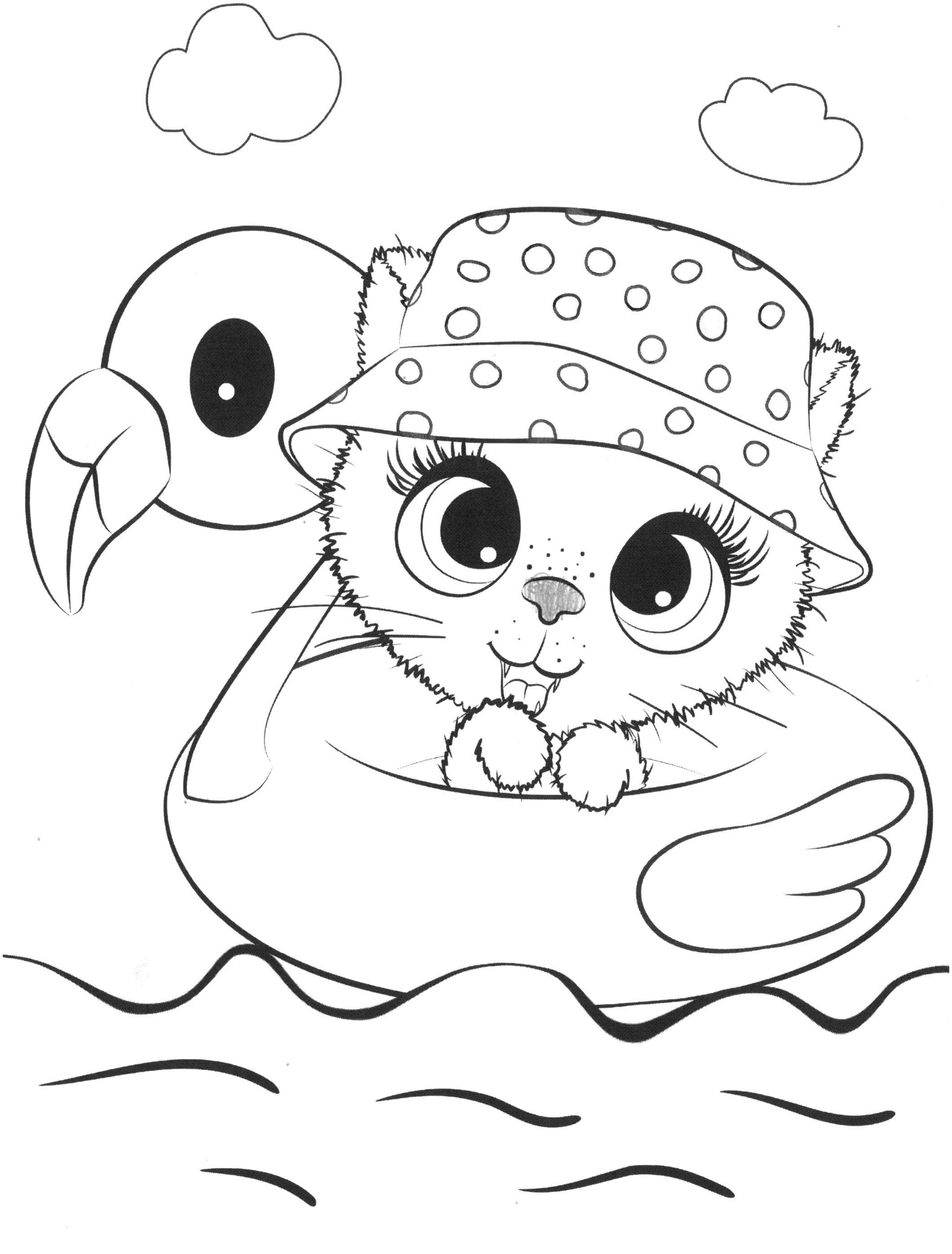

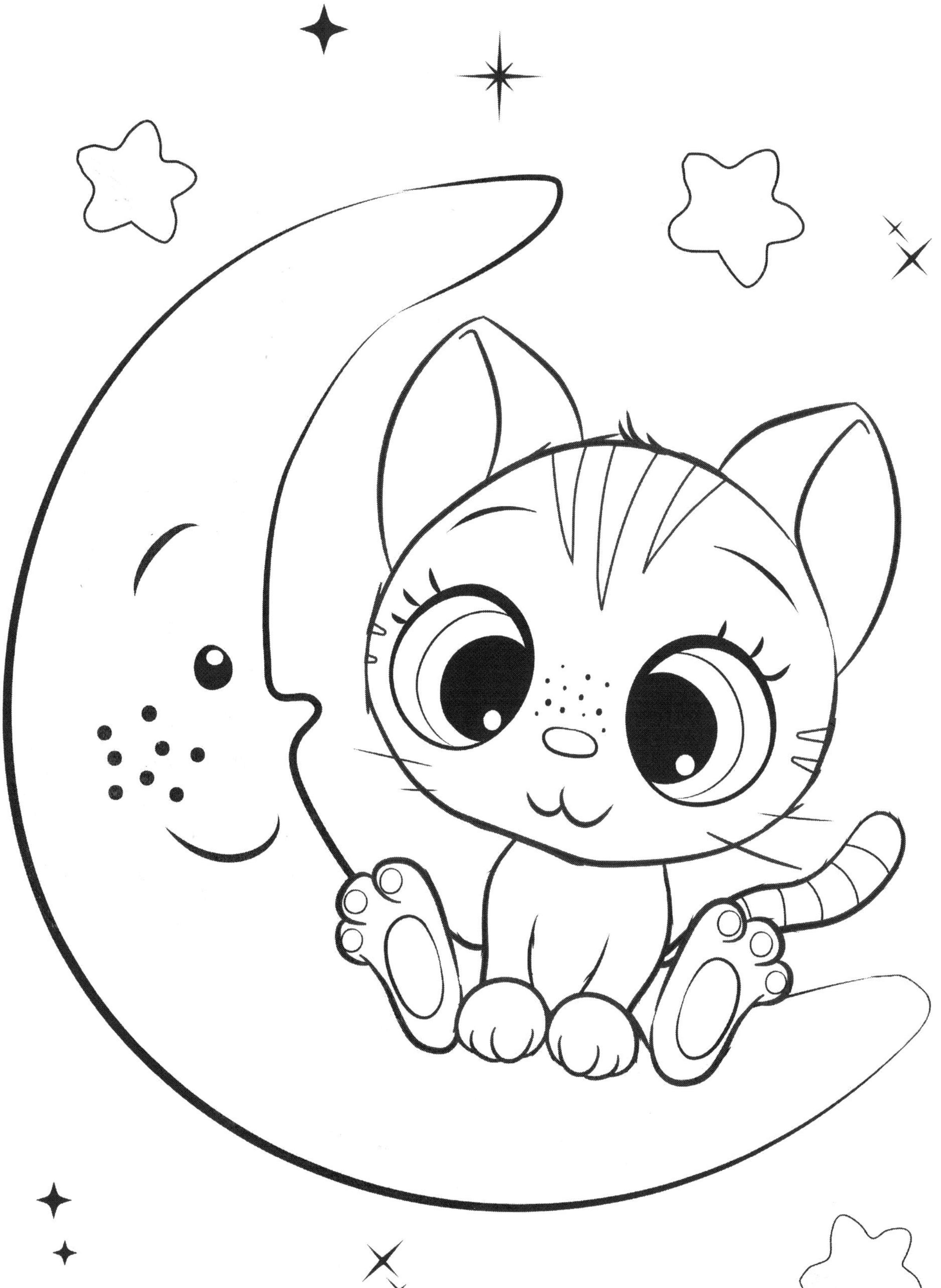

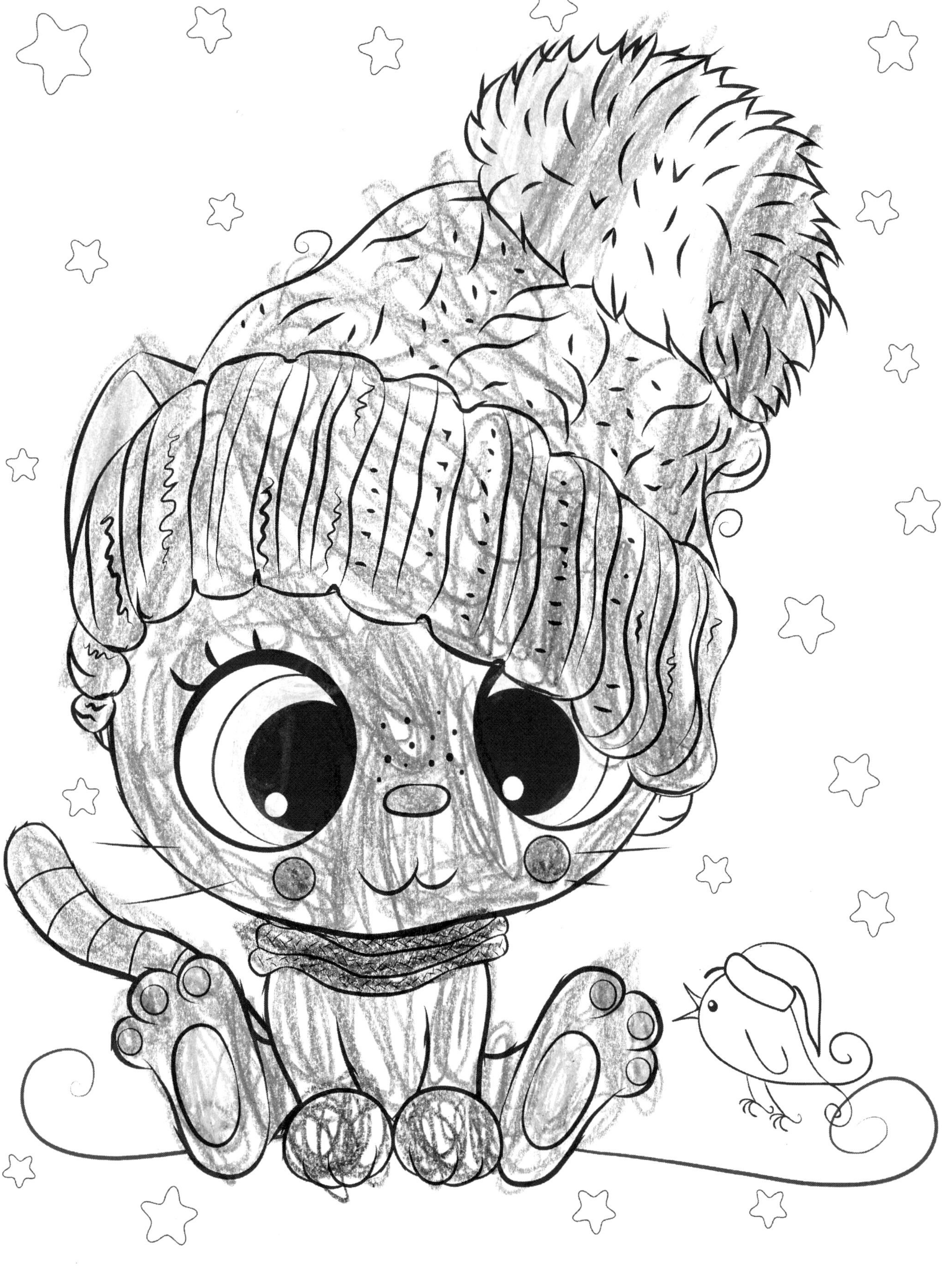

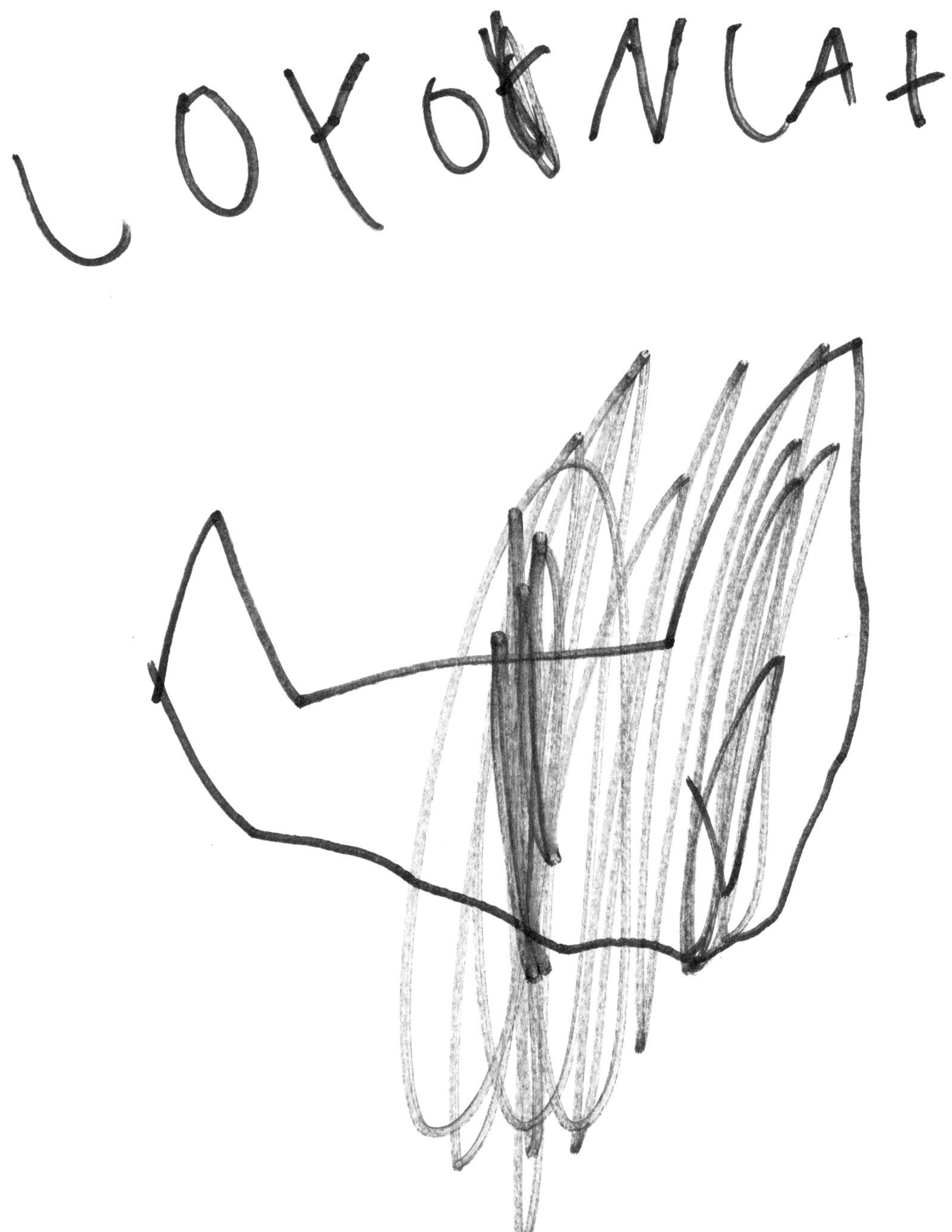

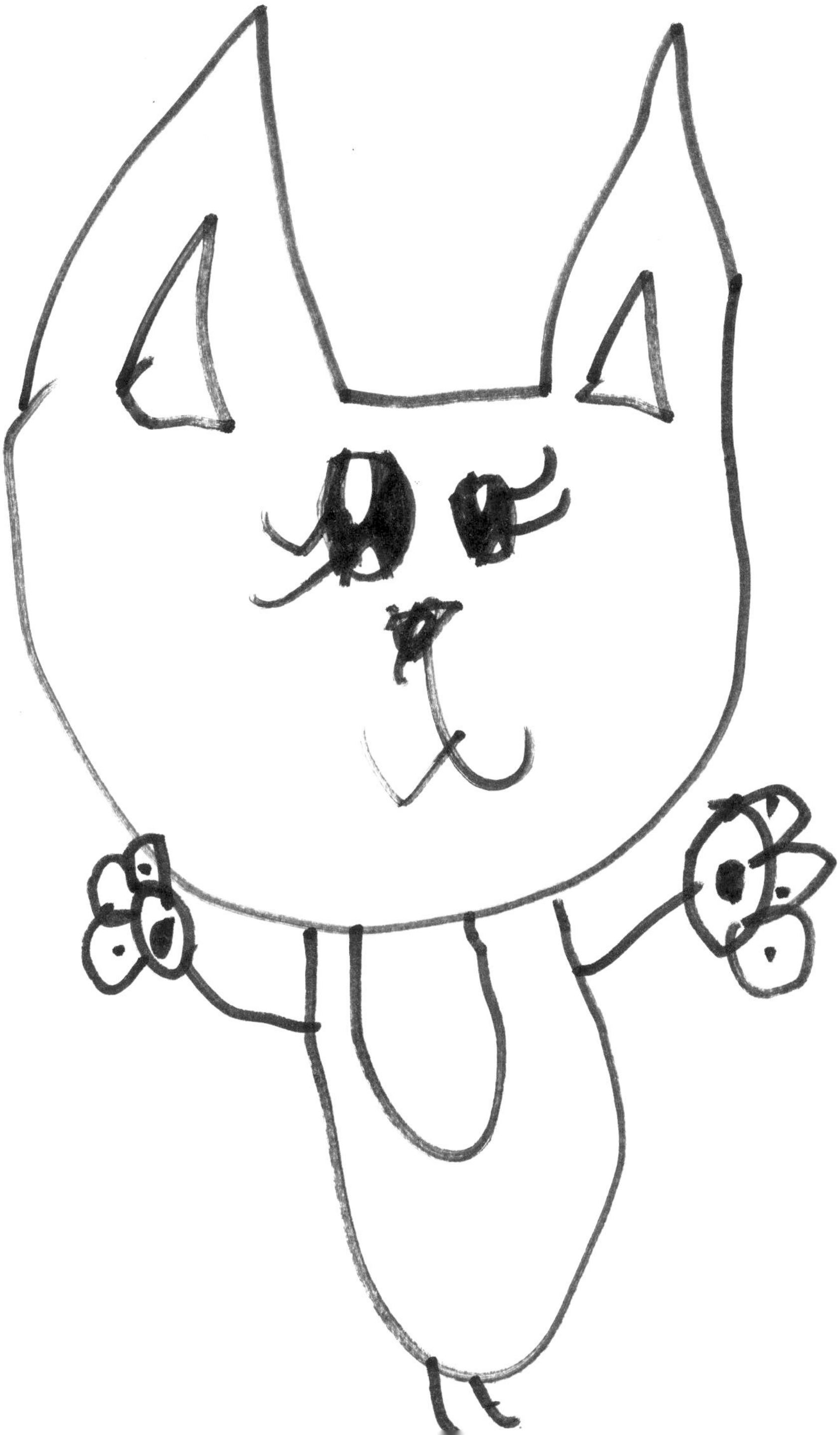

Made in the USA
Middletown, DE
14 October 2021

50090945R00035